KU-415-869

ROHAN CANDAPPA

The Retox Diet

EBURY PRESS

First published by Ebury Press in Great Britain in 2004

1 3 5 7 9 10 8 6 4 2

Ebury Press
Random House · 20 Vauxhall Bridge Road · London SW1V 2SA

Random House Australia Pty Limited
20 Alfred Street · Milsons Point · Sydney · New South Wales 2061 · Australia

Random House New Zealand Limited
18 Poland Road · Glenfield · Auckland 10 · New Zealand

Random House (Pty) Limited
Endulini · 5A Jubilee Road · Parktown 2193 · South Africa

The Random House Group Limited Reg. No. 954009

www.randomhouse.co.uk

Papers used by Ebury Press are natural, recyclable products
made from wood grown in sustainable forests.

A CIP catalogue record for this book is available from the British Library.

ISBN 0091897777

Text design by Lovelock & Co.
Cover design by Two Associates

Printed and bound in Denmark by Nørhaven Paperback A/S

For Ann

I would like to dedicate this book to my forthcoming heart attack in the hope that we can put aside our differences and, as we are fundamentally incompatible, suggest we find a way of avoiding each other in future. And, yes, I do know that we have a meeting scheduled, but would you mind awfully if we postpone it indefinitely as there is quite a lot of stuff I'd like to be getting on with.

*'Tubby, or not tubby,
fat is the question'*

William 'Triple Thick' Shakespeare
(The Lard Of Avon)

Introduction

In a world over-stuffed with so-called 'dieting regimes', there is one universal truth that few of us can deny. Diets don't work. No doubt you've tried many of them. You've weighed out mung beans. You've counted calories. And you've swallowed endless pans of tasteless soup. The only result being that you fail miserably to achieve your goals. Result, depression. Result, comfort eating. Result … Well, I don't need to spell it out for you, you big fat loser.

But all that is about to change. Because you're about to discover THE ONLY DIET THAT REALLY WORKS. It's the truly revolutionary Retox Diet. And it really works because it's not about food, it's about facts. And the fact is that you're a fat bastard because you want to be a fat bastard. And the fact of all facts, at the very artery-clogged heart of The Retox Diet, is that IT'S OKAY TO BE FAT. In fact, it's brilliant. Revolutionary or what?

A brief guide on how to use this book

Think of it as a buffet. An all-you-can-eat buffet. Dip into it when you want. Choose the tasty morsels that most appeal. And leave the rest. That's because at The Retox Diet we don't want to run your life. We just want you not to ruin it by falling for the bullshit the other dietmongers will scare you with.

Of course the other way to use the book is to whack it round the head of anyone who suggests you should go on a diet.

Enjoy!

Detox vs Retox. No contest really

The thinking behind the whole detox scam is that in the modern, western world our lives, and diets, inevitably lead to the collection of 'toxins' within our bodies. Toxins so destructive that our metabolisms can't cope. Hence we become tired, irritable, unhealthy and unhappy. The solution, apparently, is to periodically detox. This will, allegedly, re-energise us and make us healthier and happier.

What utter bollocks. Not only is it bollocks, it is also positively dangerous.

That's because if modern life is putting toxins into our bodies, then surely what we need to do is to build up a resistance to these toxins. Because without resistance we would be totally at the mercy of the toxins and far more susceptible to their vicissitudes. So any regime that works on the principle of 'detoxifying' our bodies is, in fact, only eroding our hard-earned resistances.

The Retox Diet recognises this blatantly obvious truth and consequently promotes and encourages life choices that expressly put more toxins into our bodies. And hence increases our resistance to them.

And anyway who wants to live in a world full of re-energised, healthy, endlessly happy people? Bloody hell, that would be like living in California. Or next door to Carol Vorderman. And who, in their right mind, would really want to do that?

Just chew it

Think of this profound Retox Diet invocation as a riposte to all that irritating Nike nonsense. So should you ever find yourself tempted to embark on any totally unnecessary physical challenge, just jog down to the nearest bun shop and get yourself around something cream-cake shaped.

A word of advice on so-called 'food experts'

'Food experts' are like any other experts. What I mean is that they can be wrong. For example, 'experts' used to think that the world was flat, the *Titanic* was unsinkable, and that Milli Vanilli sang their own songs.

So bear this in mind the next time you're confronted by an 'expert' on TV berating you with reasons why your current eating pattern is nothing but a recipe for disaster.

Keep a food diary

Keeping a food diary is one of the most revealing ways to uncover the true nature of your eating patterns. For a period of two weeks just record everything you eat. And that does mean everything. Read the diary back and it will soon become clear which of your eating habits leave room for improvement.

Well, that's how to do it on a conventional diet. The Retox Diet approach is somewhat different. In a Retox Food Diary you carefully note down the things that you haven't eaten. By the end of the diary-keeping period you will undoubtedly be shocked to discover how many days per week you don't have, for example, a bacon sandwich, half a packet of chocolate HobNobs, or a bathful of margaritas.

Once such a woeful and depressing pattern is written down in black and white it is far easier to confront the issue and tackle it head-on. (And mouth open.)

The genius of crisps

Truly a wonder food on The Retox Diet. A typical 34g packet of crisps contains 11g of fat. That makes the sexy little beasts almost one third fat. No wonder they taste so good. Indeed, don't think of a crisp as a snack. Think of a crisp as The Ultimate Fat Delivery System. (Second only to eating lard sliced straight from the packet.)

The thin 'friend' syndrome

Have you ever noticed that when you see a big beautiful woman out and about having a good time and living it large there is often a thin one in tow? A thin one hoping that some of the fun, glamour and all-round desirability of being big will somehow rub off on them. God, they're annoying. If one of these unfortunates should ever latch on to you, do whatever you can to ditch them and their irritating boyish hips and ridiculous tennis ball arses at the earliest possible opportunity.

An all-you-can-eat buffet is a good place to give them the slip.

How to outsmart the evil supermarkets

Supermarkets are run by cunning bastards who act as stooges for the whole 'healthy' eating conspiracy. That's why as soon as you go in you are confronted by row upon row of fresh fruit and vegetables. DON'T FALL FOR THIS CYNICAL AND EXPLOITATIVE PLOY. Refuse to conform to this prescriptive pattern of shopping. Instead, grab your trolley and scootle along to the other end of the supermarket and start from there. This way, by the time you get back to the fruit and veg you'll be so loaded up with beer, wine, frozen pizzas and Jammy Dodgers that you'll have no room left for anything else.

Why diets are, in many ways, just like blokes

There are hundreds out there, they all promise you the earth, but all they really do is screw you up, depress you and leave you curled up on the sofa full of self-pity, self-loathing, ice cream and alcohol. But despite all this you still believe that there's one out there that's going to be perfect for you. One that will make everything alright. One that you'll be with for ever.

Put it in this context and see how ludicrous it all is?

Why chips are good for you

1 Chips are made from potatoes. The potato is a vegetable. And vegetables are good for you.

2 The oil that chips are fried in is invariably vegetable oil. So it's made from vegetables. And vegetables are good for you.

3 Tomato ketchup is made from tomatoes. Tomatoes are a vegetable. And vegetables are good for you.

4 Salt comes from the sea. Hence salt is a seafood. And seafood is good for you.

5 Vinegar is made from malt. Malt comes from barley. Barley is a grain. And grains are good for you.

So, when you consider the clear, indisputable culinary evidence, it is obvious that there are few foods better for you than a bag of chips doused in vinegar, dredged with salt, then Quentin Tarantinoed with ketchup.

It pays to have heroes

Elvis in Las Vegas. Right near the end. Less of a
role model. More of a roly-poly model.

A little-known, and very useful, fact about 'aerobics'

The term 'aerobics' was popularised by Kenneth and Mildred Cooper in their books *Aerobics* and *Aerobics For Women*. And the glorious fact in question is that 'aerobics' actually means 'living, acting or occurring in the presence of oxygen'. Well, forgive me for spotting just a bit of a loophole there, but by this definition isn't everything we do 'aerobic'? Hence we can all ditch the guilt and legitimately claim that even when we're busy stuffing our faces with a box of Quality Street we are, in fact, 'doing aerobics'. Hurrah!

(Incidentally, do we seriously want to take exercise advice from a couple called Kenneth and Mildred? Shouldn't they really be instructing us on how to complete VAT returns, or knit antimacassars?)

Weight gain by numbers

If you want clear, unequivocal proof that there is a deep-rooted and ubiquitous conspiracy to make you feel bigger than you really are, all you have to do is consider the damning evidence that is women's dress sizes.

There's size 8, then size 10, then size 12, then size 14 and so on. And so on.

Well, what happened to sizes 9, 11, 13 and the rest? What great crime did they commit? Or were they just jettisoned in order to subtly and subconsciously depress the innocent dress buyer whose totally reasonable affection for the occasional kebab has caused them to go up a dress size?

Makes you think, doesn't it?

Does my bum look big in this?

Well, maybe it does. But frankly that's an approach that only emphasises the negative. Surely if your bum does look big, then that's only in proportion to the rest of your body.

The Retox Diet method of dealing with this scenario is to emphasise the positive. So if your bum does look big, don't feel down about it, because it only means that the rest of your body doesn't look big.

Now that's a fact well worth celebrating. With a cream bun.

Does my bum look big in this? (A second glance)

Now if you're still uneasy that your arse looks out of proportion to the rest of your body, there is a relatively simple, Retox Diet-approved, solution. All it takes is a bit of lateral thinking.

You see, it's not a case of your bum looking too big, it's a case of your body looking too small. The obvious solution is to bulk up the rest of your body. With a cream bun. Or three.

A fairly obvious point that all those health, fitness and diet gurus seem to have missed

Guys, we're all going to die. Maybe the real thing we should focus on isn't how long we live, but how much enjoyment we have along the way. My point being that is eighty years breakfasting on Bran Flakes really that much better than seventy years of egg and bacon?

Elasticated waistbands

Why fight the inevitable? And just between you and me, I have it on very good authority that Carrie Bradshaw has loads of the buggers secretly stashed down the back of her wardrobe.

The holistic approach to dieting

A lot of nonsense is written about holistic living. And a lot more nonsense is written about the holistic approach to dieting. You know the kind of stuff I mean. New Age mumbo-jumbo about 'living in balance' with whatever the latest thing some dippy yoghurt knitter from the West Coast of the United States of Woo-Woo has just discovered as being vital to our wellbeing. Invariably, to 'fully embrace' this holistic life you need to change your diet, your home, your daily routine, and your underpants.

The Retox Diet approach to holistic dieting is much simpler. In order to adhere to its strictures all you need do is ensure that in addition to your existing diet you eat regular amounts of food with holes in it. Hence always have in your home, or about your person, sufficient supplies of:

Doughnuts
Polo mints
Pretzels
Bagels
Hula Hoops
Aeros
Gruyere cheese

In an emergency even pizzas can be pressed into service. But only if you just consume the cheese and topping-laden middle bit whilst leaving the boring, dry crust intact.

A brief examination of the four different kinds of exercise. (And how to avoid them)

Depressingly, there are four different kinds of exercise:

aerobic   **isometric**

anaerobic   **isotonic**

Now let's be honest, none of them sound very appealing. They all sound worryingly scientific, and ever so medicinal. Should you ever have a mad moment and even consider trying any of them, quickly refer to the following list that highlights a selection of sensible places in which to veg out until the urge passes:

armchairs   **sofas**

beds   **McDonald's**

Vegging out: the alternative interpretation

Whenever you are served a meal in a restaurant or at the house of an acquaintance, make a point of sliding any vegetables that appear before you on to somebody else's plate.

Eating at work

It's a great way of spreading The Retox Diet gospel.
That's because in any workplace employing, for
example, five women, at least three of them will be
on some kind of a diet. And the other two will feel
guilty about not being on one. Your duty as a Retoxer
is to munch, chomp and graze your way through the
day on all manner of calorie-laden goodies, but only
when adjacent to these misguided dieters.

The great thing is that you won't only be doing
yourself a power of good, but you will be actively
trying to save the souls of your compatriots
ensnared by the false god of dieting.

Think of it as the modern-day equivalent of
Christian missionaries being sent into the jungles
of Africa to guide the heathen natives towards the
paths of righteousness and salvation. Instead of a
bible and a crucifix, all you're armed with is a Mars
bar and a packet of crisps. It's tough work. But it's
God's work. And your reward, in heaven, is nearer
than you think.

The Cabbage Soup Diet

On The Cabbage Soup Diet you basically live off cabbage soup. And apparently it does work. The only problem is that the side effects are far from fragrant. Which is why anyone who opts for it needs their head examined. And why we over here in The Retox Diet camp refer to it as 'The Cabbage Brain Diet'.

Why it's not your fault that you're a porker

No, it's evolution's fault. And society's. And here's why.

In the past we lived in a world where food was always in short supply. So the predominant nutritional problem was not an excess of calories, but a deficiency of them. Given this, there would be an evolutionary advantage in the ability of an individual to load up on supplies on the rare occasions when food was in abundance.

So back in prehistoric times very few people would wander round in the autumn, when food was easily found, going, 'Oh no, just a small plate of salad for me, I've got to watch my weight.' Instead it would be, 'Fill yer boots, the winter's coming!'

Now all this would still be a good approach but for one problem. Namely society itself evolved. It 'advanced'. And we developed techniques to mass produce food. And we developed technology to do most of our physical tasks. The end result is that we lead a largely sedentary life where an abundance of food is cheaply available. But, unfortunately, we are still essentially creatures evolved to survive and thrive in an environment where food is scarce.

So stop beating yourself up, because it's not your fault that you're a porker. It's evolution's. And society's.

The P.A.P. Workout

It's remarkable how many calories you burn up when completing the seemingly simple task of phoning up for a pizza. Just consider the actual complex and complicated facets involved in the task and you'll soon realise why the Phone A Pizza workout is such an effective means of controlling your weight.

1   Walking to the fridge, opening the door, realising you don't fancy anything in there, closing the door.

2   Deciding that you'd like a pizza instead. (N.B. Inexperienced Retoxers often forget that 'thinking' burns calories.)

3   Searching the kitchen drawers for the pizza restaurant menu.

4   Sitting down with the menu and working out the complex pizza options:

  THE RETOX DIET

    a. what size of pizza
    b. what type of crust
    c. what topping
    d. what additional toppings
    e. working out whether the extra toppings are
       worth the additional cost
    f. deciding on side orders

5   Making the phone call:
    - walking to the phone
    - lifting the receiver
    - dialling the number
    - placing the order
    - giving your address
    - replacing the receiver

6   Repeatedly lifting your arm to check your
   watch and wondering why the pizza delivery
   man is taking so long.

7   Repeatedly getting up from the sofa, walking to
   the window, and looking out through the curtains
   to see if the pizza delivery man is coming yet.

8   Going to the loo because you've had a couple of drinks while you've been waiting.

9   Hurriedly exiting the loo because that's the precise moment the pizza man rings the door bell.

10 Going to the front door.

11 Opening the front door.

12 Taking the pizza box.

13 Checking it's the right pizza.

14 Going to look for money to pay the pizza man.

15 Arguing with the pizza man as to why he never has any change.

16 Closing the door.

17 Going and sitting down on the sofa with the pizza box.

18 Opening the lid of the pizza box.

19 Lifting the first slice to your mouth.

20 Taking the first bite.

21 Getting up and going to the kitchen to heat the pizza up in the microwave because the bloody thing's cold.

No wonder you always feel like slumping out on the sofa after you've eaten. Frankly, you're knackered.

Celery

Why, oh why, oh why, oh why? Whose bright idea was celery? Apparently you use up more calories chewing the stuff than you get from digesting it. It kind of makes you think that maybe there isn't a God.

Celery. A second bite

On second thoughts, God, I take it all back. There is a point to celery after all. It's what you use to stir your Bloody Mary.

Why gym instructors always shout at you

It's because they have no natural authority. And shouting gives them the illusion of being in charge. And of being important. But, let's be honest, aren't they just ego-boosted, over-hyped PE teachers? And weren't the PE teachers the least highly regarded teachers at school? And gym instructors didn't even have the brains to become PE teachers. So no wonder they shout. It's because they're incredibly insecure.

Buns of steel

What more evidence do you need of the abject horror of fitness training and its end effects? I mean, 'buns of steel'? Please, enough is enough.

Buns should be made of pillow-soft white pastry, crammed full of raisins, glazed with egg yolk, lightly toasted under a grill, smothered in melting butter and anointed with a fat dollop of strawberry jam.

So you know where you can stick your 'buns of steel'.

Possible reasons why you might overeat

1 Because you're tired.
2 Because you're upset.
3 Because you're bored.
4 Because you're in the habit of grazing throughout the day.
5 Because you don't stop eating after you are full.
6 Because you're not organised.
7 Because you suffer from low self-esteem.

If you ever find yourself falling into a worrying pattern of eating 'sensibly', just refer to this list throughout the day and you will soon discover that contrary to what you may believe at the time, you do indeed possess ample resources of what we at The Retox Diet call the Motivation To Munch.

N.B. Carry on this exercise for a few weeks and you eventually will arrive at, and rejoice in, the warm and hallowed environs of Possible Reasons Why You Might Overeat, Point Eight.

Possible reasons why you might overeat. Point eight

8   Because you're a right greedy bastard.

T.A.R.F.P.

Dedicated Retoxers will know this rule by heart.
And more hardcore Retoxers often have it tattooed
somewhere on their inner thigh. It is, primarily, a
rule to be remembered, restated and, ideally, loudly
proclaimed every time you eat out in a restaurant.
So, repeat after me:

There's Always Room For Pudding

No sweat

Why do people in gyms insist on wearing their sweat with such pride? Stick the same people, in the same state, on a crowded tube train and all the other people on the train would, rightly, be disgusted. But back in the gym these louts parade around and preen themselves like Naomi Campbell sporting the latest Galliano on Milan's catwalks, their every move declaring:

'Look At Me! Look at my GORGEOUS SWEAT!'

Bizarre.

Never forget

Never forget that if God, in his infinite wisdom,
had really wanted us to take exercise, he would
never have invented the TV remote control.

Why society's even more to blame

Society's responsibility for our generally far from fit state goes beyond the development of mass-produced food and a sedentary lifestyle. That's because society has evolved into an increasingly complex psychological set-up. So much of it, from the macro-scale of global politics, to the micro-scale of the minutiae of our lives, seems beyond our control.

Our relationships with our family and friends are no longer simple. Our work environment is often a source of conflict and uncertainty. And the perception that others have of us has become increasingly important. But, perhaps most critically of all, the perception we have of ourselves has become a fluctuating morass of confidence and uncertainty that everyone tells you is vital to master if 'you want to be happy in yourself'.

Is it any wonder that we turn for comfort to something that has never let us down? We may have been dumped in relationships by people we love. We may have been made redundant from our workplaces on the whim of a boss. And we may have been refused entry at a club for not wearing the right clothes. But we have never, ever, been rejected by, or turned away at, the door of the fridge.

And don't we all need a friend we can rely on when everything else, and everyone else, fails us?

Take five

Each day aim to eat at least five portions of chocolate.

Fat-burning diets

Fat-burning diets are commonly held to be good for you. And we agree. After all, what easier way is there to indulge in a fat-burning regime than to have a full English fry-up every morning which, if you leave it in the pan just a little bit too long, will involve more than a soupçon of burning fat?

Yo-yo dieting: is it really the only option?

You know the plot with so-called yo-yo dieting. You go on a diet, you lose weight, you come off the diet, you gain weight.

But why should yo-yos get all the glory? Surely other children's toys deserve a look-in too? A few suggestions follow:

Hula Hoop Dieting Any diet regime that involves you inelegantly expending lots of energy but goes in a complete circle leaving you back where you started, usually with some useless bit of equipment that you never use again and end up shoving in the garage or down the back of the wardrobe.

Roller-Skate Dieting Any diet regime that starts off well but goes rapidly downhill.

Skateboard Dieting Any diet regime that is really easy to fall off. (But does let you wear baggy clothes.)

Monopoly Dieting Any diet that results in you monopolising the conversation whenever you go out with your mates with incredibly boring details of what you are and aren't allowed to eat, and how many microns your weight has gone up or down by in the last week.

My Little Pony Dieting A Cockney rhyming slang-inspired diet that involves drinking laxatives after every meal.

Barbie Dieting Any diet characterised by totally unrealistic goals.

Ken Dieting Similar to Barbie Dieting but essentially for gay men, so the totally unrealistic goals remain, but in a fabulously chic interior-designed setting.

Action Man Dieting Any diet regime aimed at MEN. Hence the emphasis will be on HEALTH, FITNESS and OH SO MACHO MASCULINITY. (N.B. Enthusiasts can often be spotted by their love of sweaty exercise clothes, their pride in striding naked around communal changing rooms and their NGSH* tattoos.)

*NGSH – No Gay Subtext Honest.

The slow metabolism vs fast metabolism debate

Don't fall for it. It's all a load of metabollocks. Instead adopt the philosophy of 'It Doesn't Matterbolism'. Eat what you enjoy, and enjoy what you eat.

Stretching

Stretching is very good for you. Apparently. And there are three basic types:

ballistic   **static**   **passive**

But if even reading this list makes you feel like having a bit of a lie down, then you would be far better off avoiding this stretching nonsense altogether and indulging instead in The Retox Diet-approved exercise of retching.

Coincidently, there are also three basic types of retching our experts recommend:

the dodgy prawn

'oh go on then just a small one, it's not as if I've got to drive anywhere tonight …'

the waffer-thin mint

Somewhat bizarrely, a good retching session actually gives the muscles across your stomach as thorough a workout as doing a hundred sit-ups.

If the government was really serious about creating a healthier nation, wouldn't they declare war on Germany?

Apparently the population of Britain was at its healthiest during the Second World War. The logical corrolary of this statement is that in order to improve the nation's health we should declare war, bring back conscription, and start tearing up the decking in the garden and use it to build bomb shelters instead.

Alternatively, we could ignore all the diets and dietary advice we've been blitzed with since 1945 and start eating bread and dripping again. For many reasons (including the need to maintain the supply of German lager in our pubs), The Retox Diet prefers Option B.

Lycra

Whycra?

And while we're on the subject of stupid types of clothing

Whose bright idea was it that what women really need is dental floss for their arses? Oh, I know, the genius who came up with thongs. Thanks mate.

Botox: an alternative approach

A lot of publicity has recently been clogging up the media on the pros and cons of Botox. Those in favour of the technique rave about its efficacy at getting rid of wrinkles on the face. Those anti it point out that what participants are doing is, in fact, injecting highly dubious – indeed, some would argue, poisonous – substances into your face in order to achieve the effect.

Luckily adherents to The Retox Diet can now achieve the desired results much more easily. And much cheaper. Admittedly the technique still does involve injecting something into the face that some health 'experts' think pose some level of risk. But as the old saying goes, no pain, no gain.

In order to get rid of your wrinkles, what you need to inject into your face, at regular intervals, are bacon sandwiches. And lots of them. Stick to this regime of 'Bloatox' and before long all facial wrinkles will be a thing of the past.

Retox thinking: it's not just a diet thing

Many people whose lives have been transformed by The Retox Diet ask whether the Retox approach can be applied to other areas of life. Of course it can. You just need to get the Retox principles into your head, then turn your attention and analytical skills to other areas that interest you. Take, for instance, the worlds of art and literature. Throughout this book you'll find just a few examples of Retox interpretation of some of the world's greatest works.

Great art inspired by food

No 1.
Julius Caesar

In its earlier drafts, Shakespeare called it *Julie Has Seizures*, and its theme was completely different. It was a heart-wrenching drama concerning the dangers of over-eating. At its climax a prone and dying Julie explains the cause of her demise with the immortal line, *'Ate two bloaters'*. Unfortunately the rewritten play was some guff about power, politics and betrayal.

Why fags are good for you

It's commonly acknowledged that if you give up fags you gain weight. So by continuing to smoke you are, in fact, keeping yourself healthy. And if you don't smoke, you really should consider starting.

Yet another glorious example of Retox logic.

Nuts and seeds as snacks

Many diets advocate the inclusion of nuts and seeds as 'tasty' snacks with which to ward off the pangs of hunger that may strike during the day. The Retox Diet also supports the usefulness of nuts and seeds being consumed for this end. But on The Retox Diet the form in which the nuts and seeds come is all-important. Hence seeds should only be eaten when baked into the crust of white bread rolls that have been crammed with a suitable filling. And nuts should only be eaten in the form of Picnic, Topic or Snickers bars. Or when heavily salted, and downed by the handful as an accompaniment to a round or four of alcoholic libations.

Food Combining

On the conventional Hay or Food Combining Diet you aren't allowed to eat carbohydrates and protein together in the same meal. The obvious Retox way around this is to have the 'meals' close together. Very close together.

Arsanga Yoga

Arsanga Yoga is the only type of yoga approved by The Retox Diet. It is a recently rediscovered science and practice that was developed over a period of thousands of years to deal with physical, emotional and spiritual development. However, what separates it from other forms of yoga is that it seeks to channel the debilitating negative energy that is often directed by females at a particular part of their anatomy towards a more positive end. And, indeed, a vastly increased end.

The teachings of Arsanga Yoga were first developed and codified in about 200BC (on a wet Wednesday afternoon) by the legendary Tibetan priestess, guru and bon viveur Dhasmai Bharmlukbeeg. However, it is only recently that Arsanga Yoga has come to the fore thanks to the advocacy of Sheri Halibut, the singer who used to be one sixth of the pop quintet The Rice Girls. (She was Fishy Rice.)

Sheri's remarkable Arsanga transformation from

hard arse to lard arse was shown off to stunning effect in the video she made for the England World Cup team song 'It's Raining, Sven', in which she cavorted around a rain-drenched Old Trafford wearing little more than a rather too small England shirt.

Positions featured in Arsanga Yoga include the Vheephee El, the Camel's Foot and the Crouching Tiger, Hidden Dragon, a brief description of which follows.

The Crouching Tiger, Hidden Dragon

This is a most advanced Arsanga stance and requires much practice. It should only be attempted after dark.

In this stance the devotee of Arsanga first meets up with a friend after work, goes for a couple of drinks, then visits a cinema to see the latest foreign-language film that all the reviews have been raving about, then falls asleep just over halfway through because the cinema's really warm, they haven't eaten anything and they can't be arsed to read the ludicrously small subtitles.

Then they wake up when people are clambering over them at the end of the movie, go and have more drinks (because it's too late to eat now), miss the last bus/train home and have to pay way over the odds to a dodgy-looking minicab driver who they have to tell not only where they live, but also how to get there, and which side of the road to drive on.

Like I said, it's not a stance for novices.

A load of Swiss Balls

Oh, come on. You must have heard of the Swiss Ball. It's a giant inflatable ball on which you roll around and do exercises. Apparently it's good for developing 'core stability'. Unfortunately it's also good for developing 'mental instability'.

However, Retox Diet researchers have discovered that a Swiss Ball workout can actually help you lose weight. Unfortunately it only works in Switzerland. That's because Switzerland is a very mountainous country. So you slip on your lycra lederhosen and take your Swiss Ball out into the meadow and prepare to exercise. However, you then have to watch as your Swiss Ball rolls away from your grasp as your meadow is invariably on the side of a mountain. Consequently you lose weight sprinting down the mountain to get your ball back, and trudging home again with the bloody thing.

That's why the Swiss Ball is unlikely to have much beneficial effect in the relatively mountain-free UK. (And absolutely none in Norfolk.)

Why The Retox Diet recommends salad ready washed and packed in bags

It's just common sense, really. Basically, seeing as the stuff is already in a plastic bag, it's much easier to throw away once the contents of the unopened bag go manky in the bottom of your fridge.

Why they always play pounding music in fitness classes

It's a technique beloved by evil cults the world over. And by repressive dictatorships. It's a kind of brainwashing. With music pounding in your ears, and a hyperactive rabbit shouting at you, you have no opportunity to think for yourself.

So should you ever have the misfortune to find yourself in a gym class, being shouted at while music blares at you, just imagine that the instructor is, in fact, berating you to

'Stretch forward, stretch back,
Invade Iraq!'

so as to remind yourself quite how much trouble blind adherence to a dubious, US-inspired philosophy can get you into.

Fitness classes or fascism? You decide.

Low-fat Cheddar

Don't go there. It's the thin end of the wedge.

A few thoughts on those 'handy' 200ml bottles of mineral water so beloved of the gym-going classes

Everyone knows that water in a small bottle costs twice as much as in a big bottle. But the people who drink them rationalise that they're the perfect size to carry to the gym. After all, a big bottle would be just too heavy to lug around. But surely the point of going to the gym is to exercise. And isn't one of the most common forms of gym exercise working out with weights? So, logically, shouldn't the most effective option be to buy the big bottles, lug them to the gym, and hence painlessly burn off a few extra calories?

All of which leads us to conclude that the only people that the small mineral water bottles are really 'handy' for are the mineral water manufacturers. And that's 'handy' as a euphemism for effortlessly creating vast profits. The only other people who really benefit from them are the supermodels who first championed their cause. And that's because they're the only size of bottles these anaemic stick insects have the strength to lift to their mouths.

The Biscuit Continuum.
An invaluable aid

Biscuits come in many shapes and forms. Even seasoned biscuit eaters can sometimes be confused and befuddled by the sheer variety of them on offer in the average supermarket biscuit aisle. To help alleviate this problem, the nutritionists who developed The Retox Diet have devised the Biscuit Continuum.

Chocolate
HobNobs  Cardboard*

So when confronted with a baffling selection of biscuits, just visualise the Biscuit Continuum and solely confine your attention to those close to its left-hand end.

* or Ryvita as it is misleadingly marketed

Eat your greens

Why? You're a grown-up. You don't have to.

The J.S.T.S.

I speak of the January Sales Trouser Scenario. And
it might not be a pair of trousers. It might be a
dress. Or a top. But whatever it is, the usual course
of events is clear. You go to the sales. You spot
something you really like. But they don't have your
size. But they do have it in one size smaller. So,
planning ahead, you buy them because you just
know that this will be the year when you lose
weight. And you further rationalise that buying
them will be an added incentive to stick to a diet.

Sound familiar?

Well, what about the fact that this bit of
clothing is still in your wardrobe come November,
pristine and unworn.

Sound even more familiar?

If it does, we're here to help. And The Retox
Diet solution is blissfully simple. All you need do
when confronted by the J.S.T.S. is instead of
moving down a size, move up a size. Absurd as this
revolutionary suggestion is, it actually works.

And here's how. Buy the trousers, park them in the wardrobe and every now and again try them on. Nine times out of ten they will still be too big. So instead of finding yourself depressed because you haven't lost weight (as in a normal J.S.T.S.), you find yourself elated because you haven't gained weight. End result: boosted self-esteem.

Then consider the other possibility. You try the clothing on and it fits. Well, okay, you might be momentarily down a tad because you've gone up a size, but you get to wear the trousers you like. And what's more, you didn't have to pay full price for them.

Now, are you finally beginning to see what a joy the Retox approach to life truly is?

Pulses

Always remember that the place for a pulse is on
your wrist and not on your plate.

Proof positive that the Diet Industries lie to you

How often have you heard the 'fact' that a single can of Coke contains the equivalent of six spoons of sugar? But if you were to put six spoons of sugar into a glass of water the same size as a can of Coke you wouldn't be able to drink it because it would be sickeningly sweet. So what, exactly, are these 'alleged' six spoons of sugar doing?

Great art inspired by food

No 2.
'The Scream' by
Edward Munch

Not many people know this but the
original title for this masterpiece was:
*'What do you mean there's
no chocolate left?'*

How much water should you drink a day?

Apparently it's six to eight glasses. Which works out to be about two litres. Strangely, not that long ago no-one ever mentioned that you had to drink so much of this tasteless, joy-free liquid every single day of your life. But that was way back in the days when everyone drank water direct, and almost cost-free, from the tap. Then bottled water suddenly started appearing on the scene. Bottled water that cost, relatively speaking, a fortune. Then, by some miracle of happenstance, scientific 'research' started to appear that suggested that we weren't drinking anywhere near enough water. Coincidence?

The forbidden fruit

Contrary to popular belief, fruit is not banned on The Retox Diet. That's because even the most dedicated Retoxer will occasionally find themselves tempted by fruit. After all, it is no accident that Eve tempted Adam with an apple. (And, apparently, a couple of melons, but no-one seems to mention that these days.)

The only proviso that The Retox Diet nutritionists add is that it is how the fruit is prepared that is all-important. And to this end they have developed the instructive and easily remembered FBJG rule. This stands for Fruit Bad, Jam Good. Repeat this mantra over to yourself a couple of times a day and soon it will become second nature to you. Then, whenever you are tempted by the supposed 'delights' of the fruit bowl, you'll reach for the jam jar instead.

And if you do find your self-discipline weakening while you're out and about, remember that usually you're not far from a McDonald's, where Retox-approved fruit pies (that delightfully appear to have been deep-fried) can easily be purchased for a very reasonable price.

Why fags are good for you: a second puff

A lot of nonsense has been written by people who should know better about cigarettes being bad for you. Some scaremongerers have even gone so far as to push the ludicrous theory that cigarettes can kill you because they give you lung cancer!

I mean, if this truly was the case would the government really allow their open sale in this country? Would they be morally comfortable with the implications of raising taxes from something that is killing their citizens? And would they let the tobacco companies have free and largely unregulated access to the burgeoning markets in the Third World?

Of course not.

Step classes?

Stop classes. Far more sensible.

Relationships with food. Do they all have to be bad?

How often have you heard it said that someone has a 'bad relationship' with certain foods? Some even go so far as to say that their relationship with, for example, alcohol is 'abusive'.

At The Retox Diet we just say that such thinking is far too negative. Surely it's time we examined, catalogued and indeed celebrated the alternative relationships that are possible and, we would argue, far more common with food?

Alternative relationships you can have with certain foods in your life

In love
In lust
Having a crush on
Having a long-term relationship with
The one-night stand
The bit on the side
The drunken fling that you hate yourself
    for in the morning
The ex
The transitional
The holiday romance
The childhood sweetheart
The marriage
The divorce

So don't believe the lie that the only possible relationship you can have with food is a bad one. Because you deserve so much more.

Organic?

Snore-ganic.

Squash

Always remember that it's a drink, not a game.

Flotation Therapy.
The Retox Diet angle

Many of the more New Agey diets promote the use of pampering techniques as a way of rewarding yourself for sticking to their depressing strictures. For example, many recommend Flotation Therapy. This is where you enter an enclosed darkened space and lie in warm bath of water filled with salts and minerals to achieve a blissfully undisturbed forty minutes of sensory deprivation.

But, let's be honest, isn't this just a bath in the dark with a whole box of Radox thrown in and the door locked? So when you look at it in this light, isn't it both easy and cheap to recreate at home? But for the added Retox effect we recommend that the money you save by opting for DIY flotation should be invested in a decent bottle of red wine to sup whilst you soak.

In fact, imbibe the whole bottle and not only will your sensory deprivation be more complete and enjoyable than that generated by a session in a conventional flotation tank, it will also last far longer than forty minutes.

N.B. The only possible downside is that you might fall asleep in the bath and drown. But, hey, nothing's perfect.

The simple solution to the 'What should I wear to the gym?' dilemma

Don't go to the gym.

THE RETOX DIET

Get them steaming

Should you ever mistakenly find yourself in a gym and inadvertently wander into a steam room, the correct Retox response is to stand in the doorway, fanning the door back and forward, and say:

'God, it's so steamy in here –
someone should open a window!'

This is bound to elicit a cheery response from your fellow steamees.

Height-to-weight charts

Consult these charts and you're always too heavy
for your height. But look at it another way and
surely you're just too short for your weight? A
situation that can be easily rectified by investing in
a decent pair of high-heeled Jimmy Choos.

The F-Plan Diet

There is a Retox alternative. We call it the
F-Off Plan Diet. It is, as you have no doubt
guessed, less of a diet and more of an
expression to use when anyone suggests that
you should go on a diet.

The Retox Diet video

Oh, okay, we haven't really developed one yet. But it is in the pipeline. In the meantime we recommend that you get hold of a copy of Bruce Robinson's masterpiece *Withnail And I*. Then whenever you are feeling at a low ebb, stick it in the machine and embark on the Withnail Workout.

The instructions are very simple. All you have to do is match the film characters' on-screen drinking. Every time they have a drink, you have a drink. Simple though it sounds, it really is a strenuous workout – one designed to push your stamina to the limit. So best not attempt it on an empty stomach. And get a takeaway vindaloo in beforehand. (And try not to arrange anything important for the day, or indeed week, afterwards.)

Yoga: a little-known fact

Is it any coincidence that the word 'yoga' is an anagram of the word 'agony'?
(Well, it is if you slip in an extra 'n'.)

At parties don't think of it as a buffet, think of it as circuit training

This really is a fairly advanced technique and should only be attempted when you are confident about your ability to cope.

All too often when confronted with a buffet at a party, your performance can be depressingly unimpressive. A plate is taken. A few choice items selected. Then, due to the oppressive, brainwashing, dietically correct conformists, some salad is added. Then you go and sit down and eat.

Pathetic.

How do you even hope to achieve any worthwhile results like that? Instead, adopt an approach that visualises the spread as the gastronomic equivalent of circuit training.

Scan the spread. Mentally note all the good stuff. Then give yourself three minutes' concentrated effort on each dish before moving on to the next one. Then do three minutes there. Then move on to the next one. And so on. And so on. And don't slacken off. Do the whole circuit. No matter how difficult it gets.

And never forget 'When The Going Gets Tough, The Tough Get Pudding'. You'll thank yourself in the long run.

Another fact that is all too often hushed up

Dieting is 100% fatal. Everyone who goes on a diet dies. Makes you think, doesn't it?

The importance of food supplements for your health

Like other diets, we recognise the importance of food supplements in maintaining a healthy balance of nutrients when you change your eating patterns.

The following is a list of food supplements that have been scientifically analysed by the Retox nutritionists and thus can be safely consumed *in addition* to your daily Retox meal regime.

Retox-Approved Food Supplements
Jaffa Cakes
Mars bars
Popcorn
Salted peanuts
Pork scratchings
Lard

This list is far from exhaustive.

How important is it that you warm up before you start?

It is vital, vital, vital that you warm up before you start. Otherwise you could easily find yourself eating cold leftovers. And anyway, let's be honest, it's all you really use your microwave for, isn't it? So always warm up the leftovers before you start eating them.

(Hold on, you didn't think I was talking about exercise, did you …?)

Is food a substitute for love?

No, love is a substitute for food. And a pretty poor substitute at that.

Never listen to what your body tells you

That's because your body can be a right lying bastard.
For example, you know when you're in a restaurant
and you've already gorged yourself on bread, starters
and a main course with all the trimmings? Well, for
many people at that point their bodies tell them that
they are full up. Indeed, you often hear these people
saying, 'I couldn't eat another thing.'

Then the waiter brings the dessert menu over.
And they spy something decidedly chocolately that's
whispering ever so softly 'eat me'. So they order it.
And they eat it.

Now, obviously, if they were, as their bodies were
alleging, full up, no more food would have gone in.
But it did. So, and equally obviously, their bodies were
telling porkie pies and working to their own secret
agenda. And that's why you should, when it comes to
the whole 'full-up' scenario, always take what your
body tells you with a pinch of salt. (And ideally a
pinch of salt sprinkled on a large bag of chips.)

Muesli. The unpalatable truth

There is something undeniably fascistic about muesli. For a start it's brown. And ugly. And hails from a part of Europe not really famed for its embrace of the joys of democracy or multi-culturalism. Indeed, even the act of eating the stuff involves a chomp, chomp, chomping action of the jaw that rhythmically echoes the goose-stepping marching beat of the jackboot.

Then there's the whole dubious philosophical side to the stuff. Muesli will keep you pure. In body and mind. It will keep you regular. It is cleansing. It purges your body of undesirable elements. And it sets you apart from others who indulge in breakfasts that they endeavour to actually enjoy. Yes, muesli is the breakfast of the True Believer.

But very few people today are aware of its despicable history.

Muesli was the invention of the 1930s fascist

leader Sir Oswald Muesli. While outwardly a somewhat respectable figure, Sir Oswald was, in fact, as mad as a bagful of one-eyed cats trapped in a spin dryer. He wanted nothing more than to turn Britain into a brown-shirted and brown-trousered (for obvious reasons) nation of intolerant, super-fit, puritanical fascists. And muesli was his weapon of choice.

But fool that he was, he underestimated the common sense and common decency of the British working man. So when Sir Oswald and his cohorts marched through the East End of London exhorting the masses to eat muesli, he was confronted, appropriately enough in Cable Street, by a phalanx of Eastenders who gave the hateful oaf and his followers the thrashing they so richly deserved and chucked the muesli in the Thames. The victorious Londoners then repaired to the local cafes for the traditional Breakfast Of The Free.

That's why egg, bacon, a fried slice and a tea with two sugars isn't just food. It's a political declaration of our rights as individuals to be individuals and to lead lives free from oppression, hate, and the control of those who are supposedly better than us who want to tell us how to live, what to think and what to eat.

So let us all regularly rejoice in the glory of The Full English Breakfast. And banish muesli from our shores for ever.

The G-Plan Diet

This is, as its very name suggests, the next stage on from the F-Plan Diet. It has been devised by Retox nutritionists. It is a rigorous programme that really needs to be strictly adhered to if you are to reap its full rewards. But its strictures are simple. The key elements are that every Sunday you get up late, cook and eat a full-on roast dinner, then embark on a prolonged workout session with the Sunday papers whilst lounging on stylish Scandinavian sofas and armchairs.

Jackson Pollock and his shocking relevance to dieting

Here's yet another reason why so many conventional diets are, when you get to the bottom (and I use that word advisedly) of them, dishonest. That's because none of them make any mention of one of the most distressing side effects of their dubious nutritional regimes. I speak, of course, of the J.P.T.P. – the Jackson Pollocked Toilet Pan.

The problem is that if you disrupt your normal pattern of eating your digestive system can all too often get confused. And throw a wobbly. The end result is that when you do visit the smallest room in the house, the pristine porcelain will often end up looking as if a particularly raucous stag party has indulged in a well-oiled paintball fest. With the most attractive splatters of 'paint' clinging everywhere, including that blind spot of the pan where the flushing water never sets foot.

Now why on earth would conventional diet books make no mention of this very delightful turn of events? Well, frankly, it is because they are moral cowards and deep down have a despicable aversion to accepting the consequences of their actions.

The alternative to
Mr Pollock

Of course, there is an alternative end result of some diets to the J.P.T.P. That's where, despite your best efforts, let's just say the canvas remains blank. For day after day after day.

Very minimalist. Very unpleasant.

Why three times a day all Retoxers should get down on their knees and prostrate themselves in the direction of Stonehaven in Aberdeenshire

It's where they invented the deep-fried Mars bar.

Wholemeal pasta?

Yet another favourite of conventional diets that all sensible people should be advised to avoid. Mind you, its very name should forewarn you of the delights that are in store. The reason being that the second you take the first mouthful of the stuff the following thought will appear, unbidden, in your head:

'Bloody hell, I've got to go through a *whole meal* eating this reconstituted woodchip.'

The Hip And Thigh Diet

We recommend the somewhat self-explanatory 'Chip And Fry Diet' instead.

Fruit teas: the tasteless truth

Imagine getting a bowl of potpourri, pouring boiling water over it, leaving it for what seems like half an hour, then drinking the resulting lukewarm brew. Who in their right mind would do that? So why fall for the fruit tea farrago?

'If it ain't hurtin', it ain't workin'

More patent bolleaux from the keep-fit fanatics.
Surely if it's hurtin' it's time to stop.

THE RETOX DIET

Cardiovascular exercise

Definitely a type of exercise to avoid. Far better to put yourself through a 'Bacardiovascular Workout' instead.

This is where after a cocktail-fuelled night on the town you and your white rum befuddled brain try to work out who you are, where you live and why your trousers are on back to front.

Isn't it time we brought back the tea trolley? (Another crucial Retox Diet campaign)

Come on, you captains of industry out there. I mean, aren't you forever looking for inexpensive ways to prove to your employees that you really do believe in the blatant lie that *'our staff are our greatest asset'*? And that you understand that 'staff welfare' is something more complex and important than making sure that at least one of the cubicles in the toilets has got loo roll?

So how hard can it be to:

1   Hire a little old lady in a polyester housecoat.

2   Buy a trolley (with at least one dodgy wheel) that takes up most of the room in the lift.

3   Fill a vast urn with tea twice a day and position next to it a polystyrene cup full of sugar.

4   And have a tray of slightly stale-looking sticky buns to accompany the whole glorious affair.

The major added benefit for you, apart from raised morale, would be that your staff would be far less likely to 'pop out' from work just to get a little something to keep them going mid-morning or mid-afternoon.

I mean, what's the alternative? Let them nip out whenever they want to the local Prat A Manger where they might even be tempted by a salad or something granary.

Honestly, do you really want that on your conscience?

Great art inspired by food

No 3.
The Taj Mahal

Popular misconception has it that the breathtaking Taj Mahal was created as a tribute to, and a mausaleum for, Shah Jahan's dead wife. Well, all we can say to that is get a grip.

We have it on good authority that the Taj Mahal was, in fact, built as a tribute to an Indian restaurant on the Balls Pond Road where said Shah would regularly enjoy a particularly robust Rogan Josh washed down by a bucketful of Cobras.

Hypnotherapy. An alternative

Many people can attest to the efficacy of hypnotherapy in helping them break the cycle of self-harming behavioural patterns. This often involves being hypnotised, and whilst submerged in the hypnotic state, having alternative patterns of behaviour suggested.

The Retox Diet scientists have studied such techniques and adapted them to our own philosophical approach to life. What we recommend is that should you constantly find yourself adopting a 'healthy' lifestyle, involving the likes of salad and exercise, you turn for help to the technique that The Retox Diet has exclusively developed called 'Chipnotherapy'.

Chipnotherapy is a complex approach that involves at least twice a week sitting down in a calm and soothing environment, letting all extraneous thoughts drift out of your mind, whilst having a trained Chipnotherapist gently wafting a fat, golden chip back and forth in front of your face, softly repeating the following mantra that has been carefully translated from ancient Greek (Cypriot):

'Dooyoowan saltanvinegar onat?'

Continue the programme for several weeks and you'll soon be amazed by the transformation in your life. And your waistline.

THE RETOX DIET

A word of warning

Mizuna. Red Chard. Summer Bibb. Oak Leaf.
Endive. Romaine. Lollo Rosso. Frisee. And Grosse
Blonde Parasseuse.

They are ALL types of lettuce. Avoid.

But surely people who adopt a 'healthy' lifestyle and cut out all the things that are 'bad' live longer?

No, no, no, no, NO! It just seems that way to them. Because their lives are so incredibly dull, worthy and devoid of pleasure. So don't be fooled by all the 'living longer' propaganda. And hold firmly to the desirability of one of the key Retox Diet mantras:

Tuck In, Pop Off

After all, no-one really likes people who hang around too long at a party.

And here's the other problem with living longer

The big sell on so-called 'healthy' living is that it helps you live longer. While this may well be the case, the problem is that the extra years you gain aren't added on to the start or middle of your life, but the end. So you gain more time being old.

That's more time being old in a society where the consumer-driven economy that rules over us sees you pretty much as an afterthought. And more time being old in a society where the health care that you will increasingly need is becoming ever more expensive.

Take just this single example of the warped world in which we live. Statistics now show that it is possible, because of the increasing 'health' of the nation, that people could easily live twenty-five or more years after they retire. Mention that figure to any group of people and I guarantee that the response of nine out of ten of them will not be 'Hurrah! I'm going to live such a long time!' but 'Oh my God! Will my pension be big enough? Will I have to sell my house to pay my medical bills? Will I end up as a burden on my children?'

Given all this, doesn't the Retox lifestyle, which gives you a fairly good chance of pushing up the daisies ahead of the rush but having a high old time en route, sound like the most sensible of options?

Banoffee Pie*

* Nothing in particular to say about it. It's just great to think about every now and again.

The perfect six-pack.
A six-step guide

1 Get into jogging clothes.
2 Get out of the house.
3 Get into the car.
4 Get down to the off licence.
5 Get a six-pack of Bud.
6 Get drinking.

Positive visualisation

If used correctly, positive visualisation can be a powerful tool in helping you stick to The Retox Diet. Every day clear a little time and psychic space in your hectic schedule to sit down somewhere you know you will remain undisturbed. Then close your eyes and visualise your ideal meal. And visualise it as comprehensively as possible.

Start with the cocktail that you contemplatively sup whilst munching your way through a bowl of nuts. Then visualise yourself at the restaurant table where bread and olives and individual butter ramekins are immediately brought to you. Then delight in the fact that you're with a group of compatriots where the pathetic 'Does anyone want a starter?' heresy isn't going to be an issue. Then order the wine. Two bottles of each. (It saves time.) And stare the waiter out when he asks if you'd like a bottle of water with it. Then work your way through your order. Starters. Main courses. Side dishes. And, of course, some serious puddingness.

(With dessert wine.) Then chuck in a morsel or two from the cheeseboard. (With port.) And round it off with coffee with cream. (With brandy.) And half a packet of high-tar fags.

Like I said, a powerful tool. Use it wisely.

A few thoughts on Sophie Dahl

Traitor.

(Oh, okay, it's only one thought, but it kind of says it all, doesn't it?)

The Beverly Hills Diet?

We suggest The Benny Hill Diet instead. This is, in truth, less of a diet and more of a workout. And it is particularly recommended for short, tubby gentlemen. The key elements are a large serving of innuendo, followed by a speedy training run after a well-proportioned lady whose outer garments accidentally fall off.

THE RETOX DIET

The exercise bike as the perfect metaphor for the fitness craze

You pay a fortune to buy one. Or to use one down the gym. You get on it looking a mess. You peddle furiously. And when you get off it you are in exactly the same place as you were before, only you look even more of a mess. And the only thing you've lost is half a stone of cash.

What Retoxers can learn from Tsun Tszu's writing on 'The Art of War'

Never give up. Even when the forces ranged against you seem unconquerable do not lose hope. Just think laterally. And turn what at first seems to be your enemies' strength into a weapon with which to attack them.

Such wisdom from the ancient Chinese master was originally focussed on the waging of wars. Subsequently, diplomats and politicians adopted his teachings. And now they are all the rage with a host of highly motivated and highly successful businessmen.

Well, we at The Retox Diet think that the rest of us have much to learn too. All it takes is a little imagination. Which is why we applaud the work that so many of you out there are already doing with tracksuit bottoms.

After all, what could be more emblematic of a life so seriously out of kilter that someone actually buys clothes specifically to exercise in? And what more horrific example of this behaviour could there be than the 'tracksuit' so beloved of the hated PE teachers of your youth?

But then again, what could be more inspiring than the efforts of those of you out there who have taken on this symbol of oppression and, realising that tracksuit bottoms are surprisingly comfortable and can stretch to accommodate all manner of waistlines, have wrested them away from the fitness fanatics and, both symbolically and practically, claimed them for the common man (and woman) to slob around in at leisure.

We salute you. You are heroes one and all.

The only sport of which The Retox Diet really approves

Sumo wrestling.

Oh, hold on a minute, there's actually another sport we approve of as well

Darts.

Counting calories, and calories that don't count

Einstein said that everything was relative. And he was bloody clever. What that means for the dedicated Retoxer is that it's not just the actual number of calories that count, it's their relationship to your ongoing life that really has an effect. So juxtapose food with activity, environment and your physiological, psychological and emotional states and you will find that certain calories, eaten at certain times, in certain ways and for certain reasons, just don't count.

THE RETOX DIET

Calories Don't Count:

1 If you're depressed.
2 If you're really happy.
3 If you're really drunk.
4 If you eat it standing up at the fridge door.
5 If you eat it straight from the packet/tin and don't put it on a plate.
6 If it's eaten after a hard day at work.
7 If you're finishing off what your kids haven't eaten.
8 If it's party nibbles.
9 If it's funeral buffets.
10 If it's eaten on the way back from the gym.
11 If it's eaten to cheer yourself up after you've gone out shopping for clothes and discovered you've gone up a size.
12 If your very sensible desire not to waste food forces you to eat stuff from the fridge that's about to pass its eat-by date.
13 If it's eaten in the car.
14 If it's something your mother brought over when she visited.

15 If it's crispy skin eaten while carving a roast chicken.
16 If it's chips nicked from someone else's plate.
17 If it's chocolate eaten at certain times of the month.
18 If it's the three bottles of red wine you glug down with your mate to keep her company the night after her bastard of a boyfriend has dumped her.
19 If it's a special treat that you've really, really, really earned.
20 If it's Friday.

This list is far from comprehensive, but it does give you a good idea of the general principles involved.

Doing the Marathon, Retox style

This really requires some serious training before you attempt it. Indeed some experts reckon you need at least six months' preparation. You need to start slowly and build up your stamina bit by bit. And don't get disheartened if it's heavy-going at first. Persevere. Stick to your guns. And little by little you'll get there. Should you need a further incentive to achieve your goal, why not get your family and friends to sponsor you and do the whole thing for charity?

And then the glorious day will come. The day when you stand tall, proud and ready to take the final challenge. The challenge that will mark you out as more than just one of the run-of-the-mill people around you. The challenge that, till your dying day, will enable you to look at yourself in the mirror and say, 'Yeah, I did it. I've got what it takes.'

Twenty-six Marathon bars in one day. Now how many people can say that they achieved that?

The Retox Diet way to effortlessly increase the amount of water you drink during the day

It's simple really. Ice is made of water. And a single cube of ice contains one fiftieth of your recommended daily intake of water. And a typical gin and tonic usually contains two cubes of ice. So drink twenty-five gin and tonics throughout the course of a day and you will have effortlessly imbibed your recommended daily intake of water.

Why fresh food is a con

Fresh food only contains the food itself. Nothing has been added to it. And not only are there no additives, there are no preservatives either. Now common sense tells you that additives add something to your food, and preservatives help preserve you. So why on earth do people continue to allow themselves to be short-changed by fresh food that has neither additives nor preservatives?

Junkie chic. An alternative

Open the pages of any high-fashion mag and before long you'll come across pictures of some pre-pubescent, flat-chested, hipless waif with scruffy hair, gawky legs, and eyes as glazed and as lifeless as a Monday morning mackerel's on a dodgy fishmonger's slab. Apparently this is 'junkie chic' and is something to aspire to. Mmmmm. Nice.

At The Retox Diet we would like to suggest a far more sensible and indeed, attractive, alternative. Junk food chic. To achieve the look, all you need is a baggy sweatshirt, a bag of french fries, and a smear of ketchup dribbling off your chin.

The latest New Age technique from the USA

It's LA Stone Therapy. This revolutionary therapy attempts to create a oneness with your body that is both physical and spiritual by having heated basalt and chilled marble stones placed on 'energy points' on the body. Apparently it's very popular with the movers and shakers in Hollywood.

At The Retox Diet we prefer LA Stoned Therapy. In this therapy you attempt to create a oneness with your body that is both physical and spiritual by consuming loads of drugs. Apparently it's very popular with the movers and shakers in Hollywood. (And also explains why many of them can't stop moving and are constantly shaking.)

Brown rice: a tastier, Retox Diet alternative

Cook some ordinary white rice. Smother it in HP sauce.

On language, and how the forces of evil try to control it in order to control us

The war against us is waged on many fronts. The Diet Industry will use any tactic, stoop to any level. For example, they have realised that the way to convert some of you to their cause is not by the full-frontal assault, but by proffering a reassuring hug. Hence they have invented the concept of 'food intolerances'.

Their evil logic goes that perhaps the reason you are in the state you're in isn't because you're a greedy bastard with no self-respect, but because your body is 'intolerant' to certain foods. Aaaah! Now isn't that a comforting thought. It's not your fault, it's your body's fault. And by shifting the blame like this your enemy suddenly appears to be on your side. So you warm to them. And become susceptible to their blandishments to change your diet and your lifestyle.

Well, all we can say is, don't fall for it. Or should you be confronted by the dubious propaganda of 'food intolerances', wade into the linguistic fray with the brand new concept we've invented of 'diet intolerances'. As in:

> *'Oh yes, I did try it, but it didn't really work for me because I've discovered that my body is Atkins intolerant.'*

Language. It's a powerful weapon. But with practice we can wield it just as skilfully as they can.

There's much that Retoxers can learn from the ancient wisdom of the Cockerknees

Brown bread = Dead

That river in Africa

In this touchy-feely, tree-huggingly sensitive new world in which we live it is a commonly accepted truth that to be 'in denial' is pretty much the ultimate self-harming behavioural pattern. But isn't being on a diet all about being in a perpetual state of denial?

You constantly have to deny yourself the things you want to eat, drink and smoke. And you have to deny the fact that what you really want to do after work is not go down the gym but slob out on the sofa with half a tub of Häagen Dazs, a large Baileys, and two back-to-back episodes of *Sex and the City*.

Surely such all-encompassing 'denial' can't be good for you?

The freshly blended fruit juice scam

In oh so fab 'n' groovy health food emporia all over the country, freshly blended fruit juices are sold in ounces. But you pay for them in pounds. And when you sit down and work out the actual cost of what you've bought, you realise that you could have purchased several weeks' supply of fruit for the price of a single glass. What good value. And the bloody stuff isn't even fizzy!

The hidden dangers in exercise equipment

Should you ever have the misfortune to find yourself on a gym induction, about the only useful piece of advice you'll get is that even the simplest piece of equipment can be misused. What's more, if you do use the equipment incorrectly you run the risk of doing yourself serious damage.

There is, of course, one sure-fire way of ensuring that you never misuse a piece of gym equipment. But by now you're probably way ahead of me and know exactly what we're going to suggest. Congratulations. I can see our work here is almost done.

Munches

Another excellent Retox exercise. The simplest
Munch to attempt is the Packet Of Crisps Munch.
This involves munching your way through a whole
packet of crisps. And not the low-fat kind. That
fools no-one.

At the other end of the spectrum is the
L.K.W.E. Munch*. But this really should only be
attempted by the experienced. Late at night. And
in clothes you don't mind ruining.

* Large Kebab With Everything Munch.

The dream that is steam

It is a sad truth of contemporary life that the modern kitchen is more likely to contain a steamer than a deep fat fryer. For many, many reasons this state of affairs is an ongoing and unpublicised tragedy that strikes at the very heart of our nation and saps its moral fibre. The fundamental problem here is that too many gullible people have been fooled into thinking that 'steaming' is a sensible way to cook food. And that 'steaming' gives food an aura of sophistication.

Well, we are here to dispel this blatant, and damaging, untruth. All we need do is break down the science of 'steaming' to reveal what an unappealing and unappetising state of affairs it really is. When something is 'steamed', all that is really happening is that water reaches 100 degrees centigrade, vaporises, then in its airborne form coats the food and cooks it. In other words, the food is cooked by little bits of boiling water. Or, and here's the naked truth, the food is boiled.

So what the enthusiast for 'steamed' food is really falling for is the spurious glamour created by nothing more than clever semantics. To prove my point just consider the following two meals:

Steamed fish and steamed vegetables

Boiled fish and boiled vegetables

Now while the grooviest of groovemongous restaurants could probably sell a shed-load of the former to the gullible stick insects that frequent it of a lunchtime, they probably wouldn't sell a single serving of the latter. But, as my little science lesson has clearly demonstrated, THEY ARE BOTH THE SAME.

You have been warned.

White wine spritzers

Never, never, never drink a white wine spritzer.
Never. Ever. And try not to associate with, or even
sit near, people who do.

Today cellulite, tomorrow what?

Cellulite, apparently, is the result of 'a build-up of wastes in specific areas of the body'. The areas in question being those which 'tend to collect fat as part of the secondary sex characteristics – thighs, hips, buttocks and so forth'.

Cellulite is also the Diet Industry's favourite thing in the whole world. That's because cellulite encourages in women feelings of disgust, self-loathing, insecurity, inadequacy, victimisation (because only women get it) and guilt. And all that from some fairly innocuous squidgy stuff that doesn't actually do much, if any, harm.

But here's the really interesting point: twenty-five years ago had anyone really heard about it? Or has it only really come to the fore over the period in which that the Diet Industries have set off on their leotarded and step-classing (or should that be goose-step-classing) march into the metaphorical Sudetenland of normal life?

Okay, so the Diet Industries may not have actually invented cellulite, but they sure as hell have launched a focussed, prolonged and unrelenting campaign of smear against the stuff. So that now even its briefest appearance gets about as warm a welcome as a bogus asylum seeker round at David Blunkett's house.

So, to spell it out, the Diet Industries love it because it is ubiquitous, hard to shift and (thanks to their good offices) loathed. Which makes it perfect marketing fodder for selling you stuff that is supposed to get rid of it. It also explains why, even as we speak, the Diet Industries are secretly spending millions on research into whole new categories of 'fat' you can get paranoid about. For example:

Digilite The flabby bulges of soft flesh created between the digits of your fingers when you bend them.

Lobulard Excess chubbiness of the earlobe.

Chinfill   Hanging fat between your chin and neck.

Bedsag   A truly depressing phenomena in which once you lie down in bed your relaxing muscles allow previously controlled flesh to droop like a ripe camembert in a warm dining room.

A short exploration of how our relationship with food changes for the worse over the years

When you're young, food's primary association is with home and comfort. When you get older, and have fallen prey to the evil clutches of the diet pushers, then food's primary association is with guilt. It has turned from a pleasure to a pain. How depressing.

(Incidentally, if you're Jewish this analysis doesn't really work because for you food, home and guilt are things you can't ever separate.)

The New Age approach. (And how Retoxers can cash in.)

The New Age lifestyle has got many advocates. And even though it's all patent bollocks, some people do actually benefit from the bizarre therapies involved. So what on earth is going on? And, more importantly, what can Retoxers get out of it all?

After much examination our academics have discovered that whatever the therapy, whether it's being wrapped in slurry, having an apricot enema, or having your inner thigh-hair stroked with a Tibetan prayer-wheel doused in boll weevil essence, there are two common factors involved.

First, they are all ludicrous. Second, they are all ludicrously expensive. Switch your focus to the people who espouse the benefits of these therapies and a third common element becomes apparent. Namely, the people who say the therapies work for them invariably have more money than sense.

Combine all these facets together and it soon becomes clear how and why all this stuff works. It works by removing excess money from people who subconsciously feel that they don't deserve the cash that they've stockpiled.

Hence it is the accumulation of excess, undeserved money and its associated feelings of guilt that is screwing up their lives. And the removal of said money lifts both a psychic and emotional weight from their shoulders.

So how can Retoxers benefit? Well, think it through. All a New Age therapy has to be is:

a ludicrous   **b** ludicrously expensive

So if those are the only constraints, why not cash in and start inventing your own New Age diet therapies? And when the readies start rolling in, you should find your monthly fags, wine and bacon butty bills far easier to handle.

Fromage frais

Fromage frais can often be used in cooking as a lighter, healthier alternative to cream.

Why?

Nigella Lawson.
A revelation

Who's to say that this time around when The Messiah returns she can't be a woman?

I mean, just examine the evidence. Jewish parents. Father a practitioner of a lowly and unregarded trade (politician). And in her deeds, words and teachings she's willing to take on and confront the prevailing forces and ideologies of oppression that hold the mass of people in sway to an evil empire and false gods.

Makes you think, doesn't it?

The Celebrity Baby Diet

I blame Liz Hurley.

Apparently just seconds after the doctor had cut the umbilical cord, Liz desperately reached out her hands to the nurse. A nurse who handed over a set of weights. By the time she got back to the ward she had lost half a stone. And when she and the sprog first appeared in public she was as lean as an anorexic whippet.

So did she do this so that she could feel good about herself? Or so that everyone else, and especially women who've just had a baby, would feel bad about themselves?

Now if that last option sounds too malevolent a motivation to ascribe to someone as relatively innocuous as our Liz, well, didn't she play the Devil in her recent film *Bedazzled*?

And isn't her son called Damian …

Irritable Bowl Syndrome

Another very common food-related disorder. It is a complaint most often found among the misguided folk who opt for eating plans other than The Retox Diet. Its main symptom is incredible irritation at the muck, gloop or polystyrene packing chips that end up in your bowl as your so-called 'delicious main meal of the day'.

Great art inspired by food

No 4.
Beethoven's Fifth

Originally, it wasn't a symphony. It was a reference to the fifth stein of lager he used to sup of an evening down the pub. By that point he was so well oiled he used to sing his order:

'Bring me more beer'

And he always used to sing it to the same tune that he'd made up. Then one night the barmaid suggested he wrote the tune down. The rest is history.

Häagen-Dazs
or Ben & Jerry's?

Oh come on, work with me on this one. There's no
law against you buying both.

Join Watch Weighters

This is another simple and effective way that followers of The Retox Diet can experience rapid weight loss. The technique to be followed is outlined below:

1   Buy a really, really heavy watch.
2   Weigh yourself while wearing it.
3   Record your weight.
4   Wait a day.
5   Weigh yourself again with the watch removed.
6   Record weight and marvel at how much you've lost.
7 Buy a bucket of KFC to celebrate.

N.B. For those of you needing seriously impressive results in order to, for example, prove to a loved one your dedication to dieting, I recommend the 'Duchess Of York 17 Rolex Method'. Expensive but effective.

The importance of sticking to a balanced diet

On The Retox Diet eating a healthy balance of foods is key if you want to achieve your goals. So it's important to balance your calorific intake of chocolate with an equivalent calorific intake of boiled sweets. Though you may perceive this as hard to do, the following list of Retox-approved sweets should give you some inspiration:

> Sherbert lemons
> Gobstoppers
> Cola cubes
> Pear drops
> Cough candy
> Pineapple chunks
> Barley sugar
> Fruit bon-bons
> Everton mints
> Butterscotch

So why do you think they call it a 'deep' fat fryer?

It is because culturally, philosophically and spiritually a deep fat fryer will add meaning to your life. And here's how.

Consider the potato. It grows way down in the earth. Amongst the worms. Far from fresh air. Far from the sun. It grows fat and pale and knobbly. Not for the potato the supermodel good looks of a celery stick, or the vibrant colours and continental glamour of the red pepper. No, this fellow turns up at the party thin-skinned, pasty-fleshed, bloated and unappealing.

But take that same potato to your kitchen and wash it. Peel it. Cut it into strips. And then slip those finger-fat chunks into the deep fat fryer and something truly magical happens. It bubbles, it sizzles, it dances with delight. And in but a few minutes chips emerge.

Glorious golden brown chips. Chips that

tumble down on to a plate and dare you to eat them even though you know that they'll burn your tongue. Chips unapologetic in their confidence and vitality. Chips that (metaphorically) cry out, *'Bring It On! The salt, the vinegar, the ketchup. I Can Take It!'* And chips that when you bite into them do something far beyond the wildest dreams of even the most sophisticated of foods. Chips that make you happy.

Forget Laurence Llewelyn, forget Trinny and Susannah, forget St Paul hitchhiking to Damascus: if you want a real transformation, with substance, with meaning, with true spiritual power, just look at what a deep fat fryer can do to a potato.

A pain in the grass

Some diets proudly proclaim the health-generating properties of various grasses in a balanced diet.

Grass? Are they serious?

Even the most callow Retox Diet novice knows that the only thing to do with grass is sit on it whilst enjoying a full-on *Wind in the Willows* style picnic*. Or smoke it.

* A *Wind in the Willows* style picnic comprises, in Mole's glorious words, of, 'coldchickenncoldtonguecoldhamcoldbeefpickledgherkinssaladfrenchrolls-cresssandwichespottedmeatgingerbeerlemonadesoda-water …'

Jogging

Not many people know this but the guy who first popularised jogging died of a heart attack. While out on a run. At thirty-seven*.

* Okay, this isn't in its strictest sense 'true', but it's a damn fine rumour that we ought to have a fair old crack at spreading around.

Pilates

Sorry, but that's a typographical errer. The actual strand of body conditioning associated with The Retox Diet that concerns us here is Pielattes.

This nutritious and invigorating snack combines a latte – the milky, over-expensive coffee – with a pie of your choice. As an aid to rapid weight gain, a daily Pielatte is an invaluable tool. My own particular favourites are the Apple Pielatte, the American-influenced Pumpkin Pielatte, and the good old British Pork Pielatte.

All you need to create your very own Pielatte is a nearby Starbucks, a well-stocked fridge, a powerful blender and an iron stomach. Enjoy!

Oily fish is good for you

Everyone knows that this is true. But only The Retox Diet points out the obvious, glorious corollary of this. Cod is a fish. And down the chip shop they fry it in oil. Vast amounts of which gets absorbed by the batter. Therefore cod in batter is an oily fish. So eat a trawlerload of the stuff. You'll be doing your heart a power of good.

A weight off your mind

When on The Retox Diet try not to set yourself unrealistic goals. A safe weight gain is about one to two pounds a week. Aim for any more and you'll find that it's really hard to keep the weight on.

How much more evidence do you need that the primary aim of all diets, exercise and detox regimes is to depress you and lower your self-confidence?

Go into this so-called 'healthy' living mullarkey in any detail and before very long you'll come across the following two very startling revelations. First you are, invariably, sitting all wrong. And second, you're not breathing correctly.

Bet you thought sitting and breathing were about the only two things whose principles and practice you had a firm grasp on. But oh no, according to the so-called 'experts', you're doing it all wrong.

'If I order a pudding will someone share it with me?'

What phrase better encapsulates the truly schizophrenic state of affairs we've reached? You want the pudding. But you know you 'shouldn't' have it. So, you reason that if you have only half of it and give the rest to someone else, you are, in fact, exhibiting self-control.

Well, I don't know how to break this to you, but you're not. You're being weak. And girly.

To succeed on The Retox Diet you need to face up to your desires and embrace them. If you want a pudding, order a pudding. And eat the whole thing yourself. And do it proudly. That way you'll feel a glorious and invigorating sense of empowerment.*

---

* Mind you, this might just be a sugar rush. But, as you'd expect, we're quite keen on sugar rushes.

Diets and the deity. A point of theology worth considering

If sugar is so bad for you, why did God make it taste so good? This only makes sense if God is a mean and cunning bastard. Theologically this is quite a hard position to sustain.

Facials

Many detox programmes suggest that having a facial is a great way of both revitalising your skin and giving yourself a bit of a pampering treat as a 'reward' for having spent the last ten days living off millet, lettuce and water. Under these dubious schemes, you sit back in a dimly lit treatment room, have your face covered in a variety of creams and let the 'beneficial' effects work their magic.

Needless to say, such facials, in reality, produce very little benefit.

Far better, if you feel that you deserve a bit of a treat, to indulge in The Retox Diet-approved version. The Stuff Your Facial. This involves sitting back in a dimly lit tea room and having your face filled with a variety of cream-filled, and cream-covered, patisseries.

Needless to say, Stuff Your Facials produce very real, and very enjoyable, benefits.

Telly snacking. And why to take it lying down

Australian nutritionists have discovered that eating when lying, rather than sitting, on a sofa leads to greater over-consumption because the stomach's fullness receptors are triggered more slowly.

Act accordingly.

Why it's far more socially responsible to use the car than walk for even the shortest of journeys

It's simple really. We live in a complex and complicated society in which certain goods and services we all desire can only be equitably and economically supplied on a national basis. And the only way to fund such a system is through taxation.

Everyone knows that the tax we pay on a litre of petrol is very high. But the revenue raised pays for, amongst other things, the health service, pensions, the police and the lollipop ladies who whatever the weather help little kiddies across the road on their way to and from school. So every time you jump in your car and burn petrol on which you've paid shedloads of tax, you are in fact contributing to the wellbeing and greater good of the society around you. Hence it's those people who insist on walking to places they could very easily drive to that are the truly anti-social ones.

So the next time you pop into the car to nip down to the corner shop to get a packet of fags and you come across one of these despicable pedestrians, make sure you wind down the window and shout *'Selfish bastard!'* at them.

THE RETOX DIET

Liposuction. Maybe we're approaching it in an arse-about-tit way

After much exhaustive research, the top academics who devised The Retox Diet have come up with a radical solution that enables the majority of the world's population to gain the benefits of liposuction at a fraction of the usual cost.

All it will take is a little co-operation, forward planning, and about a pound each.

The theory goes like this. The reason most people believe they're 'overweight' is because they are constantly brainwashed into thinking that there is an ideal, slim, body shape. One of the prime ways such blatant propaganda is forced upon us is by the media's quasi-deification of skinny pop singers and movie stars.

So it's hardly surprising so many people think if only they could be the same shape, they would be happy. And for some, liposuction seems to be the answer to their woes.

The only problem is that liposuction is ruinously expensive. (And dauntingly gross.)

However, approach the problem with Retox Diet logic and another avenue of opportunity opens up. Basically there are a lot more 'overweight' people than there are skinny role models oppressing them. And if the technology exists to suck fat out of the body, it must also exist to pump it back in.

So here's the plan.

All us lard arses get together and chip in a quid each. Then we take the resulting mountain of money and hire a skilled team of ex SAS men. We instruct them to kidnap, in turn, all the oppressive, skinny role models e.g. Kate Moss, Kylie Minogue, Brad Pitt. Then we whisk them away to a secret clinic in Zurich and pay a plastic surgeon to perform Lipoblowtion on them.

Then we release them back into the world and let them get back to work.

Bean soup

Another favourite staple of various diets. The obvious question that Retoxers should consider if ever confronted by a bowl of this unappealing gloop is:

'Never mind what it's been, what is it now?'

Apparently inside every fat person there's a thin person trying to get out

Unfortunately, this is true. Even more unfortunately this person is a right miserable git who will have you drinking tasteless white wine spritzers, eating lentil and alfalfa muesli, and not only joining a gym but actually going to it even after you've done the induction.

That's why it is imperative that on no account do you ever try to let this thin person out. It's far better to keep the bastard hemmed in with custard creams and toasted peanut butter, avocado and cream cheese sandwiches.

Just a toy? I think not

Barbie's got a lot to answer for. There she sits on the shelf in the bedroom of a million pre-pubescent girls. With her ridiculously long legs. Her freakishly tiny waist. Her gravity-defying breasts. And her smug, self-satisfied, serial-killer smile.

All the while she sits there exuding an innocent air that seems to simper *'Oooh, don't worry about me, I'm just a toy'*, the malevolent she-bitch from hell is, in fact, corrupting, ensnaring and destroying the chances of future happiness of generation after generation of young girls. But we still let her stay. We encourage her into our homes. We make her welcome.

Parents, for God's sake WAKE UP and smell the anorexia! It's like coming home after a night out to find that your babysitter's selling your young daughter crack cocaine yet all you do is thank her, pay her, drive her home and arrange for her to come over again!

And finally, unanswerable statistical proof that people who go on any diet other than The Retox Diet are stupid

It is a commonly acknowledged fact that around 95% of all diets don't work. Sure, you may lose weight for a while, but before long you end up back where you started.

Well, consider how you would act if those were statistics you faced in any other area of your life. For instance, what if every morning you tried to make your way to work on a bus that 95% of the time didn't stop at the bus stop you were waiting at. I mean, how dumb would you have to be to go on waiting at that stop?

Very dumb, that's how dumb. Yet when facing the same odds people still insist on going on diets.

Diets on which they expend copious amounts of time, money, soul-searching and grief. But that 95% of the time aren't going to work.

Furthermore, consider an elaboration on this line of thinking. People often go on diets because they perceive, or have been made to perceive, themselves as overweight. Naturally this results in lowered self-esteem. Hence they diet. And 95% of the time they fail. So 95% of the time a course of action they embarked on in order to raise their self-esteem has precisely the opposite effect.

Now how sensible is that?

Whereas on The Retox Diet you can't fail.

And even more finally, a short philosophical treatise on why it's bad to lose weight

If you are successful in losing weight, then there'll be less of you. You will, in short, be less of a person. Now is that really what you want?

We at The Retox Diet certainly don't.

About The Author

Not exactly Chekhov is he? I mean a load of stupid jokes and terrible puns – what kind of way is that for a grown man to make a living? But, as the saying goes, beggars can't be choosers. And he seems happy enough. But then again, maybe his outward show of humour is but a patina of frivolity that in truth conceals the soul of a tortured artist and a well of personal sadness deeper than that really deep trench in the Atlantic that greets him every day like an abyss and that he has to face down and conquer every time he sits at his laptop and starts to write.

Maybe that's why he sometimes eats one more bun than is strictly necessary.

My personal theory, however, is that he's just a greedy bastard. But he has written a lot of books. And they are all very funny. And so, on balance, I quite like him. After all what do we really need in the world more, someone trying (and inevitably failing) to be another Chekhov, or somebody trying to increase the sum total of laughter in the world?

Or maybe what we really need is someone trying (and inevitably failing) to be another Chekhov and thereby increasing the sum total of laughter in the world.

All Ebury titles are available in good bookshops or via mail order

TO ORDER (please tick)

The Little Book of Stress	£2.50	❏
The Little Book of Wrong Shui	£2.50	❏
Stress for Success	£2.50	❏
The Little Book of The Kama Sutra	£2.50	❏
Autobiography of a One Year Old	£5.99	❏
The Parent's Survival Handbook	£3.99	❏
Growing Old Disgracefully	£4.99	❏
Christmas Stress	£4.99	❏
University Challenged	£4.99	❏
One Hundred Birthday Wishes	£4.99	❏

PAYMENT MAY BE MADE USING ACCESS, VISA, MASTERCARD, DINERS CLUB, SWITCH AND AMEX OR CHEQUE, EUROCHEQUE AND POSTAL ORDER (STERLING ONLY)

CARD NUMBER: ....

EXPIRY DATE: .... SWITCH ISSUE NO: ....

SIGNATURE: ....

PLASE ALLOW £2.50 FOR POST AND PACKAGING FOR THE FIRST BOOK AND £1.00 THEREAFTER

ORDER TOTAL: £   (INC P&P)

ALL ORDERS TO:
EBURY PRESS, BOOKS BY POST, TBS LIMITED, COLCHESTER ROAD, FRATING GREEN, COLCHESTER, ESSEX CO7 7DW, UK

TELEHONE: 01206 256 000
FAX: 01206 255 914

NAME:

ADDRESS:

Please allow 28 days for delivery.
❏ Please tick box if you do not wish to receive any additional information
Prices and availability subject to change without notice.